SCHOLASTIC

100 Super Sight Word Poems

Easy-to-Read Reproducible Poems That Target & Teach 100 Words From the Dolch List

by Rosalie Franzese

Edited by Eileen Judge
Cover design by Maria Lilja
Interior design by Brian LaRossa

ISBN: 978-0-545-23830-4
Copyright © 2012 by Rosalie Franzese
All rights reserved. Published by Scholastic Inc.
Printed in the U.S.A.

6 7 8 9 10   40   18 17 16 15 14 13

New York • Toronto • London • Auckland • Sydney
Mexico City • New Delhi • Hong Kong • Buenos Aires

Teaching *Resources*

Introduction 4
Teaching Strategies 5
Activities 8
Meeting the Common Core
State Standards 11
References 11
Dolch Word List 12

POEMS

A Park (a) 13
Me (I) 14
The School (the) 15
I Go (go) 16
Where To? (to) 17
I See the Animals (see) 18
My Room (my) 19
Feelings (am) 20
I Go In (in) 21
Here I Go! (on) 22
My Family (is) 23
What Is It? (it) 24
Animals (so) 25
Look What I See (an) 26
I Can (can) 27
Up, Up, Up (up) 28
What Goes Together? (and) . . 29
I Like Fruit (like) 30
My Bunny (he) 31

Our Class (we) 32
Where Is My Teacher? (she) . . 33
Love, Love, Love (me) 34
What Can I Be? (be) 35
Look in the Sky (look) 36
The Library (at) 37
Look at That! (that) 38
I Ran (ran) 39
In the Fall (all) 40
You and Me (you) 41
Do You? (do) 42
Setting the Table (here) 43
You Are My Puppy (are) 44
In My Room (there) 45
Where, Oh, Where? (where) . . 46
Going, Going, Going (going) . . 47
What Is It For? (for) 48
What Is It Good For? (good) . . 49
Come With Me (come) 50
My Halloween Party (came) . . 51
Getting Ready (put) 52
Some Soup (some) 53
My Picture (this) 54
On My Birthday (got) 55
I Am Not (not) 56
I Like to Jump! (jump) 57
Me, Too! (too) 58
Big City (big) 59

What Is Little? (little) **60**

Where I Went (went) **61**

I Will Go (will) **62**

Making Cookies (get) **63**

My Five Senses (with) **64**

What I Say (say) **65**

We Can Play (play) **66**

Away (away) **67**

Down, Down, Down (down) **68**

Welcome to School (your) **69**

First and Then (then) **70**

The Seasons (when) **71**

My Friends (they) **72**

I Ride (ride) **73**

What I Like (but) **74**

Who Helps? (help) **75**

What I Want (want) **76**

What the Animals Said (said) **77**

Plans (was) **78**

I Eat (eat) **79**

Who Is He? (has) **80**

A Good Day (had) **81**

Too Many Pets! (have) **82**

What I Saw (saw) **83**

Who Am I? (who) **84**

What I Take (take) **85**

Please! (make) **86**

Pizza (made) **87**

If You Give Me (give) **88**

I Like Her! (her) **89**

My Baby Sister (gave) **90**

My Dog (him) **91**

Snowman (his) **92**

Get On the Bus! (us) **93**

I Am (as) **94**

Soon, Soon, Soon (soon) **95**

We Go Out (out) **96**

Our Classroom (our) **97**

What's the Book About? (about) . . **98**

My Different Feelings (very) **99**

Fourth of July (were) **100**

Where Does It Come From? (from) **101**

What Is It Made Of? (of) **102**

Everything Is New (new) **103**

Just One More... (just) **104**

Chores (must) **105**

Oh, Well (well) **106**

I Did My Homework (did) **107**

What Do They Say? (what) **108**

Now, Now, Now! (now) **109**

How Many? (how) **110**

Snow Day (find) **111**

What I Ate (ate) **112**

INTRODUCTION

Using 100 Super Sight Word Poems as Part of a Balanced Literacy Program

Word study is an integral part of any literacy program, because it teaches children about the way letters and words look and what they sound like. Children use word-study techniques to take words apart for understanding when they're reading and put words together to create meaning when they're writing (2002, Franzese, p. 146). One essential component of word study is teaching a variety of high-frequency words (or sight words) that children need to read and write automatically. I refer to these words as "quick-and-easy" words. When students have studied sight words, they are better prepared to encounter new texts, because they can automatically read them using the quick-and-easy words they have learned. This automaticity frees them up to focus not only on new or more challenging words, but also on comprehension. The less time they have to spend trying to decode words, the more time they will be able to spend on understanding what they've read.

As a classroom teacher and teacher trainer, I recognized that children need appropriately leveled text, especially during a shared-reading lesson. Through shared reading, which takes place in a whole-group setting, "children internalize all the strategies and skills" demonstrated during a lesson (2002, Franzese, p. 15). In my teaching, I used level-appropriate poetry to reinforce new sight words that were introduced to students. It turns out that poetry is a great way to teach reading and vocabulary. The predictable, sometimes repetitive text makes the poems fun and easy to master. Plus, most poems for young learners are short, so children don't get overwhelmed with the volume of text and can, instead, focus on the target words featured in the poems. One of the biggest concerns the teachers I worked with had, though, was that they did not have a collection of simple poems to choose from when planning word study and shared-reading lessons. So, I began to write my own poems using the sight words I wanted to teach. Over the years, I have written numerous poems that have been used successfully in kindergarten and first-grade classrooms.

In this book, you'll find a wide variety of poems to enhance your word study curriculum. This collection of 100 poems targets 100 sight words, from the Dolch List, that young readers need to know. You can chart the appropriate poem that matches the word you are planning to teach during a shared-reading lesson. (I like to write the poem on large chart paper, but overheads and interactive whiteboards work well, too.) Not only do the poems focus on a specific word, but many also repeat past words that have been previously taught, reinforcing what children have already learned. For almost every line of each poem, there is a corresponding illustration that students can use for meaning cues when reading. After you've read the poem aloud to students, this rebus-style format helps readers remember the content of a line they may be struggling with, and then they are better able to recall how to read those words. I also recommend reading a poem chorally with students so that they become very familiar with it.

TEACHING STRATEGIES

Teaching Sight Words Using a Multisensory Approach

Using oral reciting, hand and body movements, and magnetic letters is a great way to help young learners remember a word.

On the first day of a shared-reading lesson, I read one of the poems to the children and discuss its meaning. I choose a poem that will complement words taught from an accompanying Big Book or from a content-area lesson. I also introduce and model any hand and body movements that I want students to use when reading the poem. This brings the poem to life and helps students make a personal and cognitive connection to the text.

The next day, I go back to the same poem and begin formally teaching the specific word that I want students to learn. I begin by spelling the word with magnetic letters on a board. I ask students to tell me how many letters are in the word, and what the first and last letters of the word are. As I pull down each letter of the word, the students recite each letter name.

Then, I call on students to practice spelling the word. One student comes up to the chart and locates the word within the poem, using highlighting tape. Another student uses magnetic letters to make the word on the magnetic board while yet another is writing the word on a wipe-off board. This all occurs simultaneously. The rest of the class is using their pointer finger to trace the word on the floor or carpet area where they're sitting. As they trace the word, students are saying the letters of the word. Once they have formed the word, they say it as they underline it with their finger, from the first letter to the last.

I also like to use a technique developed by Barbara Wilson from her Wilson Reading System. The students can use gross-motor memory by extending their arms, keeping their elbows straight and using two fingers to make the word in the sky. As the children are making the letters in the air, they say and spell the word. As Patricia Cunningham suggests in her book, *Phonics They Use* (2000), the students also chant the spelling of the word, clapping as they say each of its letters.

These techniques provide students with

sensory feedback. They see the word in the poem and check to see if it looks right. They say the word as they form it and hear the word as they speak it aloud. When students form the word on the carpet, in the air, or with magnetic letters, they are provided with a tactile experience. Using hand and body movements benefits all learners, but especially kinesthetic learners.

I recommend that every sight word studied be placed on a "hands-on" classroom word wall. In my classroom, the words are placed in alphabetical order under letter cards that include an upper- and lowercase letter as well as the same picture that represents the letter on the class alphabet chart. I write the target words on index cards, and make the cards removable, so that children can use them when they're reading and writing. If your word wall is a magnetic board, place magnetic tape on the back of each index card; for other surfaces, you might use Velcro® strips to attach the word cards. Before placing a word on the word wall, I ask the whole class which letter the word belongs under, then I call on a student to come up and place the word on the word wall. This multisensory approach to word walls is a great cognitive strategy for reinforcing new words, and the students thoroughly enjoy the activity.

Masking Poems

Another great teaching strategy is "masking." Once a poem becomes familiar, you can mask parts of the poem by covering words or letters with removable tape. This technique can also be done with familiar Big Books as well. (For an in-depth discussion on how to mask text in Big Books, see *Reading and Writing in Kindergarten*, Scholastic, 2002.) Where certain letters are masked, children must analyze context and what they have learned about the spelling of the word to identify the missing letters. Where a whole word is masked, children must use context to predict or recall the word—and spell it. Masking the text prompts cross-checking between meaning and visual cues; the child has to think about the meaning of the poem as well as recall what the word looks like. I mask high-frequency words to enable students to practice reading and writing a specific word. Some teachers also mask words with tape, then write a different word on the tape. The new word may not sound right, have a reasonable meaning, or look right within the context of the poem. Children use meaning, structure, and visual cues to predict the words that are masked by the tape.

During masked-text lessons, students identify and reflect on strategies they could use to predict text covered by the tape. At first, I demonstrate only one strategy. When children are more experienced, I include several strategies. I find it is best to have students verbalize the strategies they're using, so they internalize their skills. For example, I may ask, "Why is that the right answer? How did you know that the other word wasn't correct?"

Sample Masking Lessons

The following are examples of masked-text lessons that would be done later in the kindergarten year because they focus on a couple of strategies: integrating meaning, structure, and visual cues (cross-checking cues); and practicing reading and writing sight words.

I Am
I am as fast as a rabbit.
I am as busy as a bee.
I am as smart as a fox.
I am happy being me!

Text: *I am as fast as a rabbit.*
Mask: *am*
Strategy: Recognize a high-frequency word

The students figure out what word is missing and then write that word. They check to see if the word they wrote looks like the word that was covered in the poem.

Text: *I am as busy as a bee.*
Mask: *bee*
Strategy: Cross-checking one cue against another (meaning and initial visual cues)

Students look at the picture (meaning cue) and consider the first letter of the word *bee* (visual cue). I ask, "What word would make sense?" After their response, I ask, "What letter would you expect to see in the beginning of the word *bee*?" I peel off the first part of the word, show them the *b*, and ask, "Were you right?" I then show them the entire word.

Text: *I am as smart as a fox.*
Mask: *fox*
Strategy: Cross-checking one cue against another

Students look at the picture (meaning cue) and the beginning, middle, and end of the word (visual cue). Before peeling off the tape, I prompt them: "What word would make sense and sound right?" After they respond with "fox," I ask, "What letter would you expect to see at the beginning of the word *fox*?" I then peel off the tape showing only the *f*. Then, I follow up with, "What letter would you expect to see in the middle of the word *fox*?" After students respond, I peel off the tape to show the letter *o*. Finally, I ask, "What letter would you expect to see at the end of the word *fox*?" After they respond, I peel the tape off the entire word and ask, "Is the word *fox*?"

Text: *I am happy being me!*
Mask: *happy*; write "sad" on the tape
Strategy: Integrating meaning, structure, and visual cues

Ask a student or the class, "Is there anything wrong with the sentence?" The child should explain that the word can't be *sad* because there is a picture of someone smiling. I then say, "So, *sad* would not make sense? What word would make sense and sound right?" Students reply by saying "happy." Next, I ask, "What letters would you expect to see in the beginning, middle, and end of the word?" Once they've responded, I peel off the tape, show them the word, and ask "Were you right?" This type of activity helps students internalize the strategies and apply them to their independent reading and writing.

ACTIVITIES

Reading Center Activities Using Familiar Poems

Familiar poems can serve as center activities for children to participate in while guided-reading groups are taking place. For a quick-and-easy center activity, students can simply reread poems from earlier lessons or other poems they are familiar with. I like to copy the poems on enlarged chart tablets and let the children use pointers to promote one-to-one matching and fluency and phrasing. The following activities are from *20 Reading and Writing Centers* (2005, Franzese).

POETRY OVERHEAD

Skills Practiced
One-to-one matching
Locating known words within text
Fluency and phrasing

Materials
Overhead, overhead transparencies
Dry-erase markers

Preparation
Print poem on transparency sheet. Model before making the center available to students.

How to Do the Activity
1. Select a poem and put it on the overhead.
2. Read the poem with a pointer.
3. Circle "quick-and-easy words" with a dry-erase marker.
4. Spell out the "quick-and-easy words" with magnetic letters on a magnetic board.
5. Erase markings on the poem.

POETRY STRIPS

Skills Practiced
Sequencing text for meaning
Integrating meaning, structure, and visual cues
Reading sight words
Practicing fluency and phrasing

Materials
Business-size envelopes
Sentence strips

Preparation

1. On the outside of each envelope, write a poem that was read during a shared-reading lesson.
2. Write the poem on sentence strips, one line to a strip.
3. Draw a picture clue beside each line of the poem—both on the outside of the envelope and on each sentence strip. Put the strips in the envelope. Model the procedures before making the center available to students.

How to Do the Activity

1. Read the poem.
2. Remake the poem, using sentence strips.
3. Reread the poem to check and see if the text makes sense, sounds right, and looks right. Remind students that if they are unsure, they can look at the pictures to check line order.

GUESS AND CHECK

Skills Practiced

Integrating meaning, structure, and visual cues

Materials

Magnetic tape
Resealable plastic bags
Cardboard
Paper

Preparation

1. Write poems from shared-reading lessons on separate sheets of paper, replacing some of the sight words with write-on lines.
2. Draw pictures next to each line of text to help children read the text.
3. Put a strip of magnetic tape above each blank.
4. Mount these poetry sheets on cardboard or thick paper.
5. On separate, small cards, write each word that has been deleted.
6. Put a magnetic tape strip on the back of each small word card.
7. Make an answer key by writing the sentence with the answer filled in on a separate sheet of paper.
8. Keep everything for each poem together in one resealable plastic bag. Model the procedures before making the station available to students.

How to Do the Activity

1. Read the poem and try to figure out the missing words.
2. Read the word cards and attach the appropriate word to the blank line with the magnetic tape.
3. Check your work with answer key.

Note: Every time you finish working with a poem, you might add it to the centers and take away any poem that you feel children have mastered.

Poetry Journals

You can chart poems from shared-reading lessons, and children can copy the poems to create a poetry journal. A journal can be made using a three-ring binder or a notebook. You can also make photocopies of the poems, which children can glue or staple into their journal. They can also make their own illustrations that correspond to each line of text.

Children can take home their poetry journal once a week and reread these familiar pieces of meaningful text. This gives your students the opportunity to practice fluency and phrasing as well as good reading strategies, such as integrating meaning, structure, and visual cues. By rereading these poems, students are also practicing skills of one-to-one matching and locating known words within the text. You might also encourage children to read the poems aloud to a family member, reinforcing that school-home connection.

Homework Activities

Learning to read the poems can also be practiced as a homework assignment. Make a photocopy of the poem you are teaching, for each child to take home. The children can read the poem first, then circle specific sight words. You might also delete certain sight words from a familiar poem and have the children fill in the missing words. After they fill in the missing words, children reread the poem in order to practice fluency and phrasing. An example of a homework activity follows.

Fill in the missing words, using the word box as a guide. Then read the poem aloud.

In the Fall

I look at all the trees.
I see all the leaves.
I look at all the pumpkins.
I see them all . . .
In the fall.

In the Fall

I look _____ all the trees.
I see _____ the leaves.
I look at all _____ pumpkins.
I _____ them all.
_____ the fall.

Word box

see

In

all

at

the

Using poems in addition to Big Books to teach sight words generates a positive, fun, and multisensory learning experience for children. Purposefully teaching sight words through a meaningful context rather than in isolation more effectively helps students learn how to read and write a new word. Most important, children enjoy reading the poems and look forward to it. I believe that the poems offered in this text will serve as valuable tools and resources for language arts teachers to use in their classrooms. You should also feel empowered to write your own simple poems to support your students in the wonderful and exciting process of learning to read and write.

MEETING THE COMMON CORE STATE STANDARDS

The activities in this book meet the following Common Core State Standards for K–2 English Language Arts:

READING STANDARDS: FOUNDATIONAL SKILLS

Phonics and Word Recognition

K.3.c: Read common high-frequency words by sight (e.g., *the, of, to, you, she, my, is, are, do, does*).

K.3.d: Distinguish between similarly spelled words by identifying the sounds of the letters that differ.

1.3.g: Recognize and read grade-appropriate irregularly spelled words.

2.3.f: Recognize and read grade-appropriate irregularly spelled words.

REFERENCES

Cunningham, P. (2000) *Phonics they use: Words for reading and writing.* New York: Addison Wesley Longman.

Franzese, R. (2002) *Reading and writing in kindergarten: A practical guide.* New York: Scholastic.

Franzese, R. (2005) *20 reading and writing centers.* New York: Scholastic.

Wilson, B. (1996) *Wilson reading system instruction manual.* Oxford, MA: Wilson Training.

DOLCH WORD LIST

The bolded words are featured in the poems in this book.

a	call	**get**	kind	or	**some**	walk
about	**came**	**give**	know	**our**	**soon**	**want**
after	**can**	**go**	laugh	**out**	start	warm
again	carry	goes	let	over	stop	**was**
all	**come**	**going**	light	own	**take**	wash
always	could	**good**	**like**	pick	tell	**we**
am	cut	**got**	**little**	**play**	ten	**well**
an	**did**	green	live	please	thank	**went**
and	**do**	grow	long	pretty	**that**	**were**
any	does	**had**	**look**	pull	**the**	**what**
are	done	**has**	**made**	**put**	their	**when**
around	don't	**have**	**make**	**ran**	them	**where**
as	**down**	he	many	read	**then**	which
ask	draw	**help**	may	red	**there**	white
at	drink	**her**	**me**	**ride**	these	**who**
ate	**eat**	**here**	much	right	**they**	why
away	eight	**him**	**must**	round	think	**will**
be	every	**his**	**my**	run	**this**	wish
because	fall	hold	myself	**said**	those	**with**
been	far	hot	never	**saw**	three	work
before	fast	**how**	**new**	**say**	**to**	would
best	**find**	hurt	no	**see**	today	write
better	first	**I**	**not**	seven	together	yellow
big	five	if	**now**	shall	**too**	yes
black	fly	**in**	**of**	**she**	try	**you**
blue	**for**	into	off	show	two	**your**
both	found	**is**	old	sing	under	
bring	four	**it**	**on**	sit	**up**	
brown	**from**	its	once	six	upon	
but	full	**jump**	one	sleep	**us**	
buy	funny	**just**	only	small	use	
by	**gave**	keep	open	**so**	**very**	

A Park

A boy.

A girl.

A swing.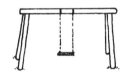

A sandbox.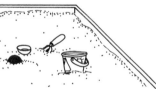

A slide.

A park.

Come play!

Me

I smile.

I read.

I run.

I jump.

I yawn.

I sleep.

ZZZZZZZ . . .

The School

The pencils.

The paper.

The crayons.

The books.

The children.

The teacher.

The school!

I Go

I **go** up.

I **go** down.

I **go** in.

I **go** out.

I **go** all about.

I **go**, **go**, **go**!

Where To?

Some days I go...

to the bus stop,

to the school,

to the park, or **to** the pool.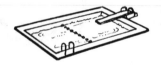

But every day,

I like **to** go home.

I See the Animals

I **see** the elephant.

I **see** the lion.

I **see** the zebra.

I **see** the bee.

I **see** the animals.

The animals **see** me!

My Room

My bed.

My bear.

My door.

My chair.

My room!

Feelings

I **am** happy.

I **am** sad.

I **am** angry.

I **am** glad.

I **am** me!

I Go In

I go **in** my room.

I see my bed.

I go **in** the house.

I see my dog.

I go **in** the car.

I see my mom.

I go **in** a lot of places!

Here I Go!

I go **on** a fire truck.

Oooh—ahhhh!

I ride **on** a bus.

Vroom, vroom!

I go **on** a train.

Choo, choo!

Oooh, vroom, choo!

My Family

My mom **is** singing.

The phone **is** ringing.

My dad **is** snoring

My sister **is** boring.

It **is** pouring.

And I am stuck inside!

What Is It?

It is round.

It can go up in the sky.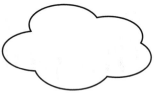

It is on a string.

What is this thing?

It is a balloon!

Animals

The snake is **so** long.

The giraffe is **so** tall.

The elephant is **so** big.

The mouse is **so** small!

Look What I See

I see **an** octopus.

I see **an** alligator.

I see **an** elephant.

I see **an** ant.

What do you see?

I Can

I am a bee.

I **can** fly.

I am a boy.

I **can** say "Hi!"

I am a horse.

I **can** run.

I am a girl.

I **can** have fun!

Up, Up, Up

The kite can go **up**, **up**, **up**.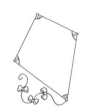

The plane can go **up**, **up**, **up**.

The bird can go **up**, **up**, **up**.

The balloon can go **up**, **up**, **up**

and away!

What Goes Together?

Bagels **and** cream cheese.

Rice **and** beans.

Bacon **and** eggs.

Food **and** my tummy.

Yummy!

<u>I Like Fruit</u>

I **like** apples and oranges.

I **like** bananas and pears.

I **like** fruit salad!

And I **like** to share—with you!

My Bunny

He hops.

He flops.

He stops.

He runs.

He is so much fun!

Our Class

We write letters.

A B C

We count numbers.

1 2 3

We go on the playground.

Yippee!

Where Is My Teacher?

It is night.

Where is my teacher?

Is **she** in the library? *No.*

Is **she** in the classroom? *No.*

Is **she** at home? *Yes!*

She is home in bed

resting her head.

Love, Love, Love

I love my mom

and she loves **me**.

I love my dad

and he loves **me**.

I love them

and they love **me**.

Love, love, love.

What Can I Be?

I can **be** a teacher.

I can **be** a doctor.

I can **be** a painter.

I can **be** a dancer.

I can **be** anything!

Look in the Sky

Oh, **look**! It is a plane.

Oh, **look**! It is a star.

Oh, **look**! It is the moon!

Oh, **look**! They are all so far.

The Library

I look **at** the books.

I look **at** the words.

I look **at** the computer.

I look **at** the keys.

I look **at** the pictures

and **at** the people.

I like to be **at** the library!

<u>Look at That!</u>

Look at **that**!

That is a butterfly flying.

Look at **that**!

That is a bird flying.

Look at **that**!

That is a bee flying.

Ouch!

That is me—crying!

I Ran

I **ran** in the park.

I **ran** on the path.

I **ran** at the beach.

I **ran** home to my bath.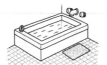

I **ran, ran, ran!**

In the Fall

I look at **all** the trees.

I see **all** the leaves.

I look at **all** the pumpkins.

I see them **all**...

In the fall.

You and Me

There is **you**,

and there is me.

I like **you**,

and **you** like me.

We are friends, **you** see.

Do You?

I like to **do** puzzles.

Do you?

I like to **do** drawings.

Do you?

You **do**?

Hey—me, too!

Setting the Table

Here is the plate.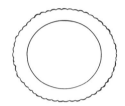

Here is the fork.

Here is the spoon.

Here is the knife.

Here is the napkin.

Here is dinner!

You Are My Puppy

You **are** furry.

You **are** small.

You **are** playful.

Here is your ball.

You **are** the best puppy of all!

In My Room

In my room,

there is one bed.

In my room,

there are two lamps.

In my room,

there are three dolls.

In my room,

there are so many things!

Where, Oh, Where?

Where is my book?

Oh, here it is!

Where is my lunch?

Oh, here it is!

Where is my backpack?

Oh, here it is!

Now I can go to school!

Going, Going, Going

Where is he **going**?

He is **going** on a trip.

Where is she **going**?

She is **going** to the sea.

Where are you **going**?

You tell me!

What Is It For?

A chair is **for** sitting.

A bed is **for** sleeping.

A pen is **for** writing.

A book is **for** reading.

A smile is **for** sharing!

What Is It Good For?

A walk is **good** for a dog.

Water is **good** for a fish.

Wind is **good** for a kite.

A star is **good** for a wish.

Come With Me

Will you **come** to the party?

Will you **come** to the park?

Will you **come** to the library

and read with me 'til dark?

Yes, I will **come**!

Great! **Come** along!

My Halloween Party

A bat **came**.

A dinosaur **came**.

A clown **came**.

A ghost **came**.

Boo!

We all ran out!

Getting Ready

I **put** my clothes in my bag.

I **put** my teddy bear in, too.

I **put** a book in my bag

and I **put** a snack in, too.

I **put** my bag in the car.

Off we go to somewhere far!

Some Soup

Put **some** carrots in the pot.

Put **some** potatoes in the pot.

Put **some** peas in the pot.

Put **some** tomatoes in the pot.

Stir it up, but be careful!

The soup is hot!

My Picture

This is my paper.

This is my paint.

This is my brush.

This is the picture

I painted just for you!

On My Birthday

I **got** gifts on my birthday.

I **got** hugs and kisses, too.

And I **got** some cards

That said, "I love you."

I Am Not

I am **not** eating vegetables.

I am **not** eating steak.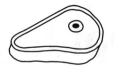

I am **not** eating salad.

I am only eating cake.

"Oh, no, you are **not**!"

My dad said.

I Like to Jump!

I like to **jump**

up and down.

I like to **jump**

in puddles.

I like to **jump**

on a trampoline

and into a tub with bubbles.

I like to **jump, jump, jump!**

Me, Too!

I can ride my bike.

Me, **too**!

I can brush my teeth.

Me, **too**!

I can tie my shoelaces.

Me, **too**!

I can clean my room.

Not me!

Big City

Big buildings are cool.

Big buses and

big trucks are, too.

The city is **big** and fun.

I like this **big** city.

Do you?

What Is Little?

A **little** seed, a **little** plant.

A **little** bug, a **little** ant.

A **little** girl, a **little** boy.

A **little** car that is a **little** toy.

Where I Went

I **went** to the left.

I **went** to the right.

I **went** up and down.

I **went** to bed—good night!

I Will Go

I **will** go to school.

I **will** go to the pool.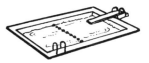

I **will** go to the park.

I **will** go home before dark!

Making Cookies

I will **get** butter and eggs.

You will **get** milk and flour.

I will **get** chocolate chips.

You will **get** a pan.

We will all **get** cookies.

Yummy!

My Five Senses

I see **with** my eyes.

I hear **with** my ears.

I taste **with** my mouth.

I smell **with** my nose.

I feel **with** my skin.

I learn a lot

with my five senses.

What I Say

I **say** *stop.* I **say** *go.*

I **say** *yes.* I **say** *no.*

I **say** *please.* I **say** *thank you.*

I **say** *hello.* I **say** *good-bye.*

I **say** so many words!

We Can Play

Come and **play** with me today.

We can **play** with blocks.

We can **play** with clay.

Come and **play**

And stay all day!

Away

The wind came

and blew my kite **away**.

The sun came

and melted my snowman **away**.

A cat came

and scared my bird **away**.

Away they went. Bye-bye!

Down, Down, Down

Go **down** the hill.

Go **down** the stairs.

Climb **down** the ladder.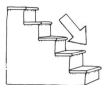

Sit **down** in chairs.

Down, down, down!

Welcome to School

Here is **your** desk.

Here is **your** chair.

Here is **your** pencil,

your pen and paper, too.

This is **your** classroom.

Welcome to **your** school!

First and Then

First your socks, **then** your shoes.

First dinner, **then** dessert.

First one, **then** two.

First hide, **then** seek.

You find me, **then** I will find you!

The Seasons

When it is winter,

I put on my coat.

When it is spring,

I plant some seeds.

When it is summer,

I go to the pool.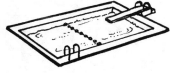

When it is fall,

I go to school.

My Friends

They like to play baseball.

They like to play soccer.

They like to play basketball.

They like to play hockey.

My friends are fun and

they love to play sports.

I Ride

I **ride** in a car.

I **ride** in a truck.

I **ride** on a bike.

I **ride** on a bus.

Oh, how I love to **ride**!

What I Like

I like skating, **but** not skiing.

I like carrots, **but** not tomatoes.

I like pens, **but** not pencils.

I like peas, **but** not potatoes.

I like a lot of things—

but not all things!

Who Helps?

Bees **help** build hives.

Ants **help** build hills.

Beavers **help** build dams.

Now I need some **help** from you.

Will you **help** me tie my shoes?

What I Want

I **want** to see flowers grow.

I **want** to hear birds sing.

I **want** to play in the sun.

I **want** it to be spring,

so I can have fun!

What the Animals Said

The cow **said**, "Moo."

The duck **said**, "Quack."

The pig **said**, "Oink."

The farmer **said**, "Shhh!"

Plans

I **was** going to ride my bike.

I **was** going to have a swim.

I **was** going to stay outside.

I **was** not going to come in.

But it rained!

I Eat

I **eat** breakfast.

I **eat** lunch.

I **eat** dinner.

I **eat** a bunch!

Who Is He?

He **has** a truck.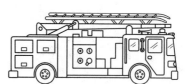

He **has** big boots.

He **has** a hat,

and he **has** a hose—

he can take it wherever he goes.

Who is he?

A firefighter!

A Good Day

The horse **had** an apple.

The horse **had** some hay.

The horse **had** a long ride.

The horse **had** a good day!

<u>Too Many Pets!</u>

I **have** a bird.

I **have** a cat.

I **have** a dog.

I **have** a hamster.

I **have** too many pets!

What I Saw

I **saw** a bear.

I **saw** some grapes.

I **saw** a pear.

I **saw** an ape.

I **saw** it all

Inside my book.

Here, have a look!

Who Am I?

I am not a bug **who**

lives in a rug.

I am not a cat **who**

sleeps on a mat.

I am not a kitten **who**

wears a mitten.

Who am I?

I am a boy **who** likes toys.

What I Take

I **take** a bite.

I **take** a sip.

I **take** a picture.

I **take** a trip.

Please!

Please **make** me a sandwich.

Please **make** it with cheese.

Please **make** it with tomato.

Please **make** it, oh, please.

Thank you!

Pizza

I **made** the dough.

I **made** the ball.

I **made** the pizza.

We ate it all!

If You Give Me

If you **give** me crayons and paper,

if you **give** me glitter and glue,

I will make some art—

and **give** it to you!

I Like Her!

I like **her** crown.

I like **her** castle.

I like **her** throne.

I like **her** dress.

I really like the princess!

My Baby Sister

I **gave** her a bottle.

I **gave** her a kiss.

I **gave** her a toy.

She **gave** me a big smile—

like this!

My Dog

I give **him** food.

I bring **him** water.

I take **him** on a walk.

I listen to **him** talk.

Woof, woof, woof!

Snowman

These are **his** arms.

This is **his** nose.

Here are **his** buttons.

Here are **his** clothes.

Hello, snowman!

<u>Get On the Bus!</u>

Do you want to

learn with **us**?

Do you want to

play with **us**?

Do you want to

sing with **us**?

Come on, get on the bus!

I Am

I am **as** fast **as** a rabbit.

I am **as** busy **as** a bee.

I am **as** smart **as** a fox.

I am **as** happy **as** can be!

Soon, Soon, Soon

When will we get there?

Soon!

When will we eat?

Soon!

When will we go home?

Soon, soon, soon!

We Go Out

We go **out** and run.

We go **out** and ride.

We go **out** and jump rope.

We go **out** and play all day!

Our Classroom

Here is **our** table.

Here is **our** art.

Here is **our** teacher.

Our class is so smart!

<u>What's the Book About?</u>

This is a book **about** cars.

This is a book **about** trains.

This is a book **about** bikes.

This is a book **about** planes.

There are books **about** everything!

My Different Feelings

I am **very** mad

when I break a toy.

I am **very** sad

when the fun ends.

I am **very** glad

when I see my friends.

I have so many different feelings!

Fourth of July

Flags **were** waving.

People **were** marching by.

We **were** having a great time.

Fireworks **were** in the sky.

It was the Fourth of July!

Where Does It Come From?

Eggs come **from** chickens.

Apples come **from** trees.

Milk comes **from** cows.

Honey comes **from** bees.

What Is It Made Of?

The table is made **of** wood.

The cup is made **of** glass.

The car is made **of** metal.

The candle is made **of** wax.

Everything Is New

I have **new** shoes.

They are not too tight.

I have **new** pants.

They fit just right.

I have a **new** pencil with a sharp tip.

And I got a **new** haircut—

Snip, snip, snip!

Just One More...

Please, **just** one more cookie.

Please, **just** one more slice of bread.

Please, **just** a little more time.

I **just** do not want to go to bed!

Chores

My mom said,

"You **must** do your homework."

My dad said,

"You **must** make your bed."

My brother said,

"You **must** walk the dog."

"Why **must** I do everything!" I said.

<u>Oh, Well</u>

I dropped my ice cream. Oh, **well**.

I fell down. Oh, **well**.

I missed the bus. Oh, **well**.

I am having a bad day.

Can you tell?

Oh, **well**! Oh, **well**!

I Did My Homework

I **did** my reading.

Yes, I **did**.

I **did** my math.

Yes, I **did**.

I **did** all my homework.

Yes, I **did**.

I **did** it all…

I am the homework kid!

What Do They Say?

What does the cow say?

Moo.

What does the rooster say?

Cock-a-doodle-doo.

What does the horse say?

Neigh.

What does the farmer hear all day?

Moo, cock-a-doodle-do, neigh!

Now, Now, Now!

Meow, meow, meow!

My cat wants his dinner right **now**.

Meow, meow, meow!

He wants his toy right **now**.

Meow, meow, meow!

He wants to be brushed right **now**.

He wants it all right **now**!

Meow, meow, meow!

How Many?

Count **how** many birds.

Count **how** many bees.

Count **how** many trees.

You know **how** to do it.

Count one, two, three!

Snow Day

Can you help me **find** my hat?

Can you help me **find** my mittens?

Can you help me **find** my scarf?

Thanks!

I am going out to **find** some fun!

What I Ate

I **ate** one jelly bean.

I **ate** two cookies.

I **ate** three ice cream cones.

I **ate** four cupcakes.

I **ate** too much!